A DAY IN THE LIFE OF A
School Basketball Coach

by David Paige
photography by Bill Smith

Troll Associates

Library of Congress Catalog Card Number: 80-54101
ISBN 0-89375-452-8   ISBN 0-89375-453-6 Paper Edition

The author and publisher wish to thank Elgin Academy, Loyola University, and Leroy Stampley for their generous
cooperation and assistance.

As he drives to work this morning, Leroy Stampley
has something heavy on his mind. He is a school
basketball coach, and today is the big game. The
winning team will qualify for the league play-offs.
But Tom, the top scorer on the coach's team, went
home sick yesterday.

Coach Stampley finds two other members of the team waiting for him in his office. They hope to get athletic scholarships to college, and want to discuss which colleges they should try for. The coach always tries to find time to talk with students about any problems they might have.

He also works to improve the physical education program in the school. When he learns that the school cannot afford to buy some special exercise equipment, he tacks a notice on the bulletin board. It tells about one way everyone can help to raise money for the equipment.

The coach changes into gym shirt and sneakers in the locker room. The game is still on his mind. He and the assistant coach have a few minutes to discuss it before the first period begins. If Tom doesn't show up by lunch time, several key plays will have to be changed.

First period is a physical education class. Coach Stampley puts thoughts of the coming game aside. Winning games is important to the team, but physical fitness is important for everyone.

Class starts with a ten-minute workout. If students do these exercises regularly, their muscles grow stronger, joints loosen up, blood circulates freely, and lungs work efficiently. The coach keeps himself in shape by working out along with his students.

Coach Stampley believes people should understand physical fitness, as well as practice it. While the students catch their breath, he explains what each of the exercises is for. He has designed his own calisthenics programs for different ages and for the different sports he teaches.

During basketball season, most of the period is spent playing basketball. At teachers college, Coach Stampley also studied baseball, volleyball, soccer, field hockey, touch football, and track and field. He coaches varsity basketball, but he teaches all the other sports.

When a student twists his ankle, the coach checks it out. Athletic coaches are trained to treat minor injuries like pulled muscles and bruises. They are also trained to handle more dangerous situations like broken bones or heat stroke. Even with the best safety precautions, a coach must be ready for emergencies.

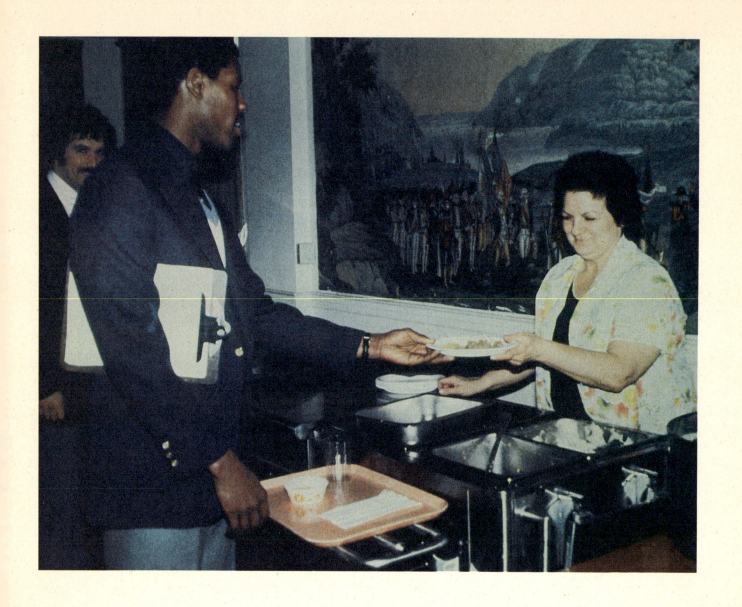

Coach Stampley often works during his lunch period. Today, he brings a clipboard with him, so he can plan emergency strategy for today's game. Besides changing several key plays, a new tactic has occurred to him. It is a surprise move, to be used in a jump-ball situation.

After lunch, Coach Stampley is relieved to see that Tom has recovered, and is back in school. The coach shares his new surprise play with Tom and his friend. The play is an exciting one; but it will not be used unless it can be practiced before the game this afternoon.

More important, is Tom really well enough to play? Coach Stampley is responsible for the well-being of his team. He questions Tom closely. Tom had an overnight virus infection. Although he still felt a little shaky early this morning, he has fully recovered now.

After lunch the coach has a health class. Nutrition is part of the course, and the subject especially concerns him. At this age, some of his students go on crash diets. Crash diets can be dangerous, he explains. If students wish to lose weight, they must still be sure they eat a balanced diet.

Classes are over at three o'clock. The team begins to assemble in the gym. The coach officially announces that Tom will play today. He tells everyone to change into gym clothes so they can have a brief warm-up session.

While the team is in the locker room, the coach takes a few minutes to talk with the cheerleaders. He reminds them that the team does not have the "home court advantage," because the game will be played at the opposing team's school. The stakes are high. The team will need all the cheering it can get.

At first, practice does not go well. The boys are nervous, forget their moves, and bump into one another. Coach Stampley is nervous, too, as he always is before a game. But this is no time to show it. He has learned to remain calm. His steadiness calms the team down, too.

By the end of the short practice session, the team is in good spirits. All their hours of work have paid off. Some players are better shooters than others. Some are better ball handlers, or rebounders, or defenders. The coach has molded these individuals into a smooth-working team.

The bus that will take the team to the game is waiting. The warm-up has eased the players' nervousness. They feel more confident now, and can joke with one another. They are eager to try the new jump-shot play in the game.

"No fooling around on the bus," the coach warns. "And when we get to the school, behave yourselves." Coach Stampley wants to win this game as much as his team does, but he also believes in good conduct. Even if his team loses, he wants the players to feel the pride of good sportsmanship.

The cheerleaders will go by car. Another teacher will drive them, because Coach Stampley always rides in the bus with the team. He will not have time to talk with the cheerleaders again before the game, so now he gives them last-minute encouragement. "We want to hear you cheering loud and clear!"

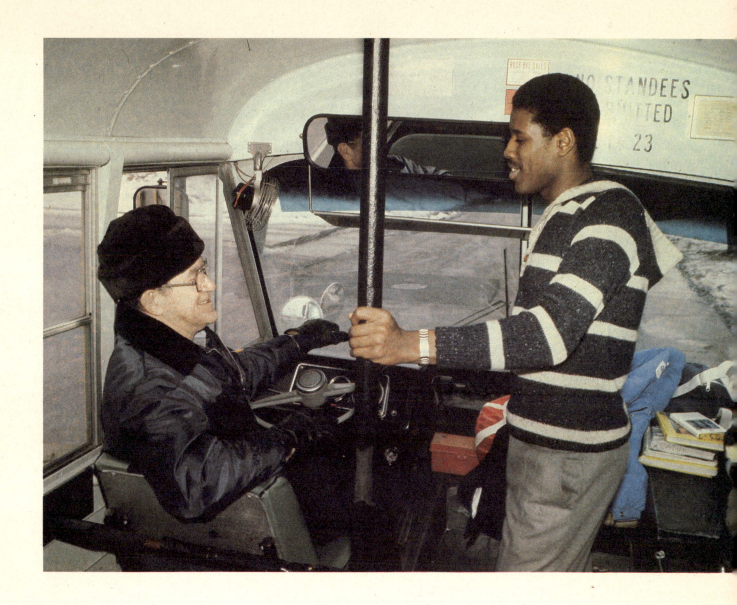

Time to go. The bus driver has driven the team to all the away games this season. He is an enthusiastic fan, and wishes Coach Stampley good luck. As they ride to the game, the coach will talk with each team member individually. It is his way of getting them to concentrate.

In the locker room, the players kid around as they put on their uniforms. But all of them are more worried than they admit. The locker room feels unfamiliar. Upstairs in the gym, the bleachers will be filled with strangers rooting for the other team.

When the team members are dressed, Coach Stampley gives them last-minute instructions. He goes over the jump-ball play again, and tells them they will have only one chance to use it. You can't surprise a good team twice. Then he gives them a pep talk to get them ready to charge out onto the floor.

Before the opening tip-off, Coach Stampley talks with the referees. This game, they warn him, will be called very closely. The coach knows he will not always agree with those calls. But he has told his team to display good sportsmanship, and he will, too. He always tries to remain on friendly terms with the referees.

The game is under way. The nervousness is gone.
Players, coaches, and referees concentrate on what
each has to do. The team gets off to a good start.
They set up their defense well. Their passing is fast,
and they work the ball skillfully. They are getting
good shots, and making them.

Coach Stampley doesn't relax, though. He calls out, encouraging his players as they go for shots. He stands up as the game becomes more and more tense. His team begins to fall behind. As the other team scores basket after basket, his players seem to fall apart.

By half time, however, the other team's lead has been reduced to four points. Now the coach changes from man-to-man defense to zone defense. He tells his team to go into a full-court press. He does his best to fire them up. Now they will really show the other team how ready they are to get back in there and play basketball!

Early in the second half, the team makes two quick baskets to tie the score. Then the lead goes back and forth several times. Now, with only seconds remaining in the game, the score is tied again and there is a jump-ball. The coach calls time out. He tells Tom that this is the time to use the surprise play.

Tom taps the ball behind him. A teammate grabs the ball, whirls around, and throws it down to the end of the court. Another teammate is there, and he is all alone. One dribble and he goes in for the lay-up. And it's good! The buzzer sounds, and the game is over!

They have won! Now they will go on to the play-offs. This has been a game to remember. Every team member feels the thrill of victory and the joy of success. For Coach Stampley, seeing them like this is one of the great rewards of coaching.